About the Author

Samual Karlin is a disabled veteran of the U.S. Coast Guard turned poet by very fortunate circumstances that took cathartic writing and made it into something beautiful. He lives with his wife and their dogs Finn and Ozzie. Samual is a first-time author hoping for a grand future in the realm of poetry and fiction. He works in the information technology field at the college he attended for some time and which helped hone rampant thoughts into poetry.

The Death and Rebirth of Affection

Samual Karlin

The Death and Rebirth of Affection

Vanguard Press

VANGUARD PAPERBACK

© Copyright 2024
Samual Karlin

The right of Samual karlin to be identified as author of
this work has been asserted by him in accordance with the
Copyright, Designs and Patents Act 1988.

All Rights Reserved

No reproduction, copy or transmission of this publication
may be made without written permission.
No paragraph of this publication may be reproduced,
copied or transmitted save with the written permission of the publisher, or in
accordance with the provisions
of the Copyright Act 1956 (as amended).

Any person who commits any unauthorized act in relation to this publication
may be liable to criminal prosecution and civil claims for damages.

A CIP catalogue record for this title is available from the British Library.

ISBN 978-1-83794-279-4

This is a work of fiction. Names, characters, businesses, places, events and
incidents are either the products of the author's imagination or used in a
fictitious manner. Any resemblance to actual persons, living or dead, or actual
events is purely coincidental.

Vanguard Press is an imprint of
Pegasus Elliot Mackenzie Publishers Ltd.
www.pegasuspublishers.com

First Published in 2024

Vanguard Press
Sheraton House Castle Park
Cambridge England

Printed & Bound in Great Britain

Dedication

To my friends, those that stayed and those that I pushed away, and most importantly, to my wife; She who stayed and showed me love.

Acknowledgements

Zach Martin without whom this would not exist. Kasey Karlin without whom the feelings wouldn't have been as firey and vibrant enough to compose this.

The Casualty Is Me

I know
I should know better
and protect myself from Death's door
but I'm always losing
and I reach for the knocker.

You know that
saying sorry
will make it all go away
but you can't.

Maybe if I roll over
and let you bull-doze on
maybe I can
learn to be happy
with that.

I should know better
I should know better
not to stand in this fire
and just walk away
but I can't.

Like a siren to Ulysses

you call to me with your
occasional sweetness
and there's no one
to tie me to the mast.

The casualty is me.

Punching Bag

You get high on my mistakes
letting your anger run wild
like the fire that destroys me
when I suggest a simple thing.
You've been building me up
just so you can knock me down.
Getting under my skin
is your greatest pleasure.
All I want is to talk,
not feel uneasy with your interactions
but you are steam rolled too.
What do you see when you look at me?
A doormat?
Punching bag?
Inhuman and not worth consideration
I would wager at the least.
Do you know what I see when I look at you?
My everything.
My future.
My tormentor.
My demon.
My hell.
But I stick around anyway,
I must love the way you hate me.

An Ode to Solitude

That's it
I'm done
I can't do this any more.
I ask for so little
but get nothing in return.
That's it
I'm done
You were once so wonderful
but now turned to stone
by your own past
that you won't let go of.
That's it
I'm done
I can't deal with this any more
affection to you is only for the dog
you hate my jealousy but fertilize it anyway.

Is this what you wanted?
A catastrophe to warrant your eternal dismay?
Well here you are,
I'll wrap it in silver just for you.
That's it
I am done.

Do You Think Yourself an Artist?

Like some great sculptor of old?
Crafting and toiling and creating?
Chiseling away at the marble of me?
I think you do.
So callously proud of yourself,
and your work.
Do you even know what you've made?
I do.
You've made doctor visits time and time and time again
when I didn't want to go
but I had no other choice.
You've made quivering terror just from leaving through
the front door,
though you would tell me to just try the window.
You've made crawling skin, and seething hatred
just from looking in the mirror.
You've made cowering nights and days,
though you would just say time to 'man-up.'
You've made purple and blue and black and yellow
like a painter strikes their brush.
So thank you,
thank you
thank you
    —fuckyou—

for these lovely gifts you've forced upon me,
remind you of anything else?

Puppet Master Acquaintances

I can't tell you from foe,
you play friendship so well.
But at the end of the day day day
I am just on your strings
dancing as you direct.

I keep trying to find the scissors,
but you've rusted and dulled dulled dulled them,
can't lose your favorite toy.

Your smile is my year's wage,
toil and boil and through the soil
to earn just a glimpse,
it's all I want want want,
but you're a scrooge.

You make me feel so small now.
Once I felt your equal,
I can hardly remember.
Like a sculptor
you chipped away way way.
All I have left,
is dancing as you direct.

Earl Grey

The loneliness inside me is a place. I go there often and just sit and ponder the universe. Sometimes it's expansive and all, while others it's more of an igloo.
I sit there and drink my tea and think of all of you
But I can't figure how to reach out in a meaningful way.
See, this all makes my thoughts so clouded, selfish and altogether blank. The light isn't on upstairs.
I would say it's the end of the line. But was there ever any line there to begin? Maybe dots and dashes, morse code you send out to me hoping I'll understand. I don't even have the right equipment, but that matters not to you.
The air here is stifling. Like my lungs don't work right. It makes it hard to do anything. So instead I do nothing. Just sit and sip my tea while movies play out in front of me showcasing the happy people I can't reach. Can't understand. I know no languages that they do. All foreign in their glee and bliss.
The earl grey is cloudy like this place. There is no honey, that would be a luxury not afforded in Loneliness. The murky waters churn in the heat, bubbling and boiling up, too hot to be enjoyed.
The glasses I wear are broken. See? I hear they are supposed to make things pretty and clear, but these

ones, these ones are thick, foggy and scratched. I can't make much out.

How's that for honesty?

Goddamn Right

I said you're scaring me.

Have mercy
I said, no don't do this.

Goddamn right
I said, this is fucked.

In this life
there is only wrong and right
black and white
darkness and light.

And goddamn right
you're scaring me
how could you?

You said, love,
but with a dagger poised high.

I didn't see it
until from my chest it sprouted,
a thistle cared for by who else
but you.

Too busy
looking at the doctor's notes
to look me in the eye,
too busy to say goodbye,
your dagger left to its lonesome.
I think I know the feeling.

Whiskey Solutions

I know this isn't a solution
but I already finished the bottle
so no point trying your hand.

Look, I'm sorry.
I am so sorry.
I shouldn't have.
But I'm terrified,
you say that this isn't me.
And you're right,
you always are.

I'm terrified
I did this to myself
worked myself
twisted and contorted myself
until an anxiety knot
resides where my heart did.

I know this isn't a solution
but I already finished the bottle
so no point trying your hand.

Listen dear,

I know what it looks like
but I swear
that this isn't
no, don't cry
this one is on me
and my other issues.
The ones I don't like talking about.

I know this shriveled mess isn't
what you expected
all I wanted was to live up to
what you thought I was.

I know this isn't a solution
but I already finished the bottle
so no point trying your hand.

Maybe I'm Crazy

Sometimes I wonder.
I was so ready to accept you
into my life
without question really
whether you wanted even to be here.

Maybe I'm crazy.
Or maybe thinking this much
about something so simple
is what is actually crazy.

Maybe I need to take a step back
and analyze this
for what it is
instead of what I want it to be.

Maybe I need to take a step back
and not block the sun
from this infant plant.

Maybe I'm crazy,
And all this stress
I've loaded onto my shoulders
is just a figment of

my twisted imagination.

Sometimes I wonder.
What do you think
goes through my head
when you look at me?

Power

I've given you so much
control over my well-being
and general happiness,
that I wonder how
I ever coped before.

Phobias

I've come to face my greatest fear.
Accept it for what it is and move on.
I'm not saying I like it,
Quite the contrary.
But it is what it is.

This time, I'm ready to die alone.

Distrust

I'm scared of losing something just found
I'm scared of what my mind has done
I'm scared I did this to myself.

You said you want to see me but you can't right now.

Maybe I'm over thinking
Tearing this apart myself
Why am I like this?

Do you care like I do?
Do you think about me like I you?
Do you want to get to know me?

You said you want to see me but you can't right now.

I believe you
I believe you
I believe you

But should I?
Are you playing games?
Do you realize what you're doing?

You said when this is all over, but not right now.
I said that's fair,
I understand.
I hope.

Blue Moon

It never starts off this way
but oh how it ends
every time, the same.

Butterflies beat their wings
against my cavernous interior.

Just like in New York, I am peaking
and the result is unprecedented.

It never starts
anywhere else
but the tips of my fingers
hungrily clawing up the length of the digits
leaping from bone to bone
crossing joints like lowered draw bridges
ignoring the flesh
and gunning for that which
is me.

I can feel you in my ears,
fiery and beating,

putting up a fight
but altogether losing
I don't know how you do it,
I've never learned the mystery.
But a master of the art,
you are
a Norse in a siege.

My knees wibble and wobble,
I feel heavier than I am.
Each flex and forward
I ache
under the newfound pressure of you.

And now through
my heart
you render me raw,
marking your victory
complete…
I'm cold

I Saw You Walking

with him
not hand in hand
but still it hurt.
Why?

I'll tell you.
You make me
no time.
I feel I am
a pauper
on your streets
begging for a moment.

I saw you walking,
you looked
lovely.

I saw you walking
with someone
that wasn't me.
Someone else
was entertaining
you.

All I want
is to be

everything.
Maybe that is
a lot to ask
this soon.
Maybe that's where
my problem lies.

It's all too soon.
too soon too soon.
I keep screaming to myself
and no one else.
But I don't know how
to turn these feelings
off.

It's all too soon

but how am I to
progress this along
without you?

I saw you walking,
but not
by my side

Confessions

I'll break it to you easy
This is hell
this is hell
Literal hell.

Your past has never
left your side
and you don't seem to care
that it's going to cloud
our future.

I'll break it to you easy
this is hell
this is hell
literal hell.

There's something
I want to ask you
but every time I look at you
I see all of them too.

There's something
I need to ask you…
Will you please
shut the fuck up
about your goddamn

past and move on
so we can have a
future?

I'll break it to you easy
this is hell
this is hell
literal hell.

Please don't
let this last
forever

Oh Pacific

Since first sight,
only you do I wish to behold;
fanciful beauty beyond
your frothy white collar.
Ever changing,
with more potency
than the seasons.

Ever changing,
but always the same.
You are reliable beyond
my expectations.

You offer me something
no one else can
or will.
I can depend on you
like none other,
I feel.
Do I dare let you in?

I wade into your
welcoming grasp
and I feel safe.
Oh Pacific,
will you keep me as yours?

I Don't Mind If You Fuck up My Life

In fact, I really just want you
to get in here and add your own flair.

I wade in shallow
and you invite me deeper,
caressing me up and down gently.

So deeper I go and all I feel is your warmth.
You are all that is life,
oh Pacific, never do I
wish to leave your depths.

Thrall

Enthralling to many
I think you to be.
But what do I know,
as I am one of them.

I can ignore what they say,
I can ignore what I see.
For you my eyes are blind.
Oh Pacific, you do me no wrong.

But this should not be so.
So many have you enthralled
to be your own,
do I wish to be one of the many?

Riptide

Everyone saw it but me.
Everyone held their tongue.
Fascinated by the show we put on.

I can't tell you from foe,
you play lover so well.
But in the end,
I am just on the ends of the line
dancing as you direct.

I've had inklings
of thoughts to find the scissors
and sever the lines,
but you dulled them with your siren song
and enthralled will I remain,
dancing only in your domain

I Do

Accept me into your depths,
I want to be yours.

I promise to cherish you always
for your beauty and your downfalls,
you are mine and I am yours.

Oh Pacific, I am your thrall.
Do with me as you please.

Through sickness and health,
I do solemnly swear
that I will uphold you
and all that you are.

I will bear true faith and allegiance
to you and you alone.
To me, no wrong
could you enact.

All orders will I obey.

You've Flown Your Colors

It never begins this way
but how the web you've woven
entraps me more
with every move.

All I wanted was to serve
and fulfil my duty
to you.
But you uncoil,
your colors flying high
like a Jolly Rodger,
my demise is on the horizon

Oh Pacific,
the whip sting you've
lashed into me
I will bear for life,
a memento from you,
I didn't know I needed.

Your scythe has left its mark,
and now I see you,
the blindness once
in my eyes has lifted
and only black death do I see

in your eyes
where once was love

Miss Murder

You've played your hand
and now my eyes are wide.
Oh Pacific, I wish they weren't.

Once your thrall,
once your lover,
Now I am betrayed
by your blood lust.

Should I have known by the wars
waged upon your territories?

Should I have known by the countless masses
I've pulled from the same depths
that once warmed my soul?

But no, I turned a blind eye
instead, only seeing the beauty you held.
Little did I know
The sirens of old were just you,
singing your song of slumber
and loving grasp
to make those of mine your own.

Miss Murder
I see you.

I Lost

All you did
was simple;
sought out your normal state
albeit too quickly
and that was enough.

I can see it;
your body turning
itself inside out,
running all over the deck,
the fluid trapped
within you
have wrecked
you throughout.

Feel it;
your muscular composure
turned fittingly
to water bed,
no human feel
left to remain.

Smell it;
the saltiness of your bile

will never leave my nose,
the smell of death pushing
into me with every
attempt to grant you
a second chance.

Taste your death;
I want to avoid this,
but your life
trumps mine
this time,
and yet the salty
seafoam death

flies from you to me.

Your salty watery fish breath
corrupted all she was
and thus it came for me
as well, finally.

All you did was simple
and my task was the same
repeat repeat repeat
half an hour went by
and like a sponge you
leaked over the deck.

The water from your lungs
did I remove,

but oh the pressure was far too great
collapsing your integrity
and stealing your humanity.

I can see it
feel it
smell it
taste your death.

Your salty watery breath
corrupted all she was,
turned her strength into
a flaccid mush under all
your pressure.

All you did was simple
and my task was the same
pump pump pump
the salty sodium sea foam poison
from your lungs
half an hour went by
and like a sponge
you just covered the deck.

I can see it
feel it
smell it
taste your death.

Your salty water breath

corrupted all she was,
stealing her naivety
and contorted it and her
until barely human.

Oh Pacific,
I trusted you,
loved you even,
and this,
this is not what I expected
in return.

All you did was simple
And my task was the same
And I failed failed failed
you.
I tried. I really did.
You scarred me. Took me under with you.
Tangled in your web of lines I drowned with you.
You took me down to her,
She I couldn't stand to see.
And stare blankly back
did she,
my once love, but
I failed failed failed you
I'm sorry.

Push-up Bra

This probably comes out of
a raging anxiety,
but here we go anyway.
You never dress up for me.
And that's okay.
But today you donned clothes
you only pull out to impress,
and yet you were gone
all day. Without me.
So who are you trying to make smile?
Who needs to be impressed in your life,
that I know not of?
Who's eyes need to be drawn to your breasts?

Distant you have been for weeks,
and that's okay.
But then something clicked,
and the blinders came off.
I saw how weird you had become,
how little you wanted to do with me.

To You I'm Just a Man

To me you're all I am.
But that's not true is it?
I am so much more,
to you, to me.
Control over myself is
all I ask.
I wrestle this from
the universe
with my verse
but it feels as if
that's the most
I can muster.
My thoughts race and
run amok in my brain palace
disrupting the delicate furniture
until I rest in shambles.
Putting words down every day
only about you
because you're my universe,
But I forget that I can be there too.

Chasing Nightmares

I don't know if I dreamt this
or let my imagination take control
and hallucinated the whole thing
but last night was hell in my brain.

Watching you walk away,
normally a pleasure,
but this time not.

Of my own machinations,
I forced you out
and off you ran.
No fight,
no argument,
but simply gone.

And this scares me,
what if I lose control
and let this become my reality?
I wouldn't last much longer.
This was a dream
or maybe a nightmare.

You were everything to me

but in the end, I was just a man to you.
I loved you with everything I had,
but in the end, it was too much.

You spoke in tongues
with your love language to me,
if you even had one.
and I spoke plainly
but in the end, it was too much.

I feel like I'm doing you a service,
forcing you to walk away.
All the while killing
the most precious part of me.
In the end, this was all too much.

The Storm is Coming

This is going to hit me
like a hurricane
but it's worth it
to weather this storm.

I can't be myself with you
and when I am
you explode
ripping my head off.

I'm a hydra
playing masquerade
around you.

Is it too much to ask
to be happy with myself
when I am around
my chosen person?

All the Love in the World

and you couldn't spare me a moment.
'I don't need to be touched'
you would say.

Sometimes I feel the same
but you didn't reach out anyway.

Loving you was like
speaking in tongues,
not something I can do.

All the love in the world
and maybe I was the problem
not believing you when you said
'I do.'

Second Chances

Maybe you deserve one.
I don't know how to tell.
Maybe I was the problem
all along.

But in these nights I feel I spent alone
despite you there
somehow warming the sheets
despite the ice in your chest
I couldn't help but wonder
if this is what I deserve.

And more times than not
I talk myself into
thinking this exactly that
and I earned nothing better.

If this is how it is
that's fine,
the consequence is mine.

You Changed

Starting off
you were all I wanted.
Like I made you in a computer,
perfection all the while.

Maybe that was too high a standard
because you started falling short.
Spiraling into who you really are.

I had to bury myself alive
to let you flourish,
all the while
making you think I was content.

Is this what I deserve?
A life I feel I earned?
Look into yourself and tell me
we are not the same,
we are different.

I the romantic
you the glacier.
But you didn't start off that way
did you?

Villain

You make me feel
so evil
when I love you.

You kept pushing me to the edge
that I surrendered myself
and forgot it all.

I wanted this life
for myself, for you
that I surrendered myself.

Like a villain
I fell
for you, from myself

Waves

You come and go
in waves.
Making me question
my peace of mind.

Death Is All Around

I'm falling
and calling
out to you
but do you hear me?
Death is all around
welcoming me into
its macabre grasp.
And I can't help
but wonder
if this is the answer
I have been looking for.

Crowds

I think you've been running with the wrong crowd.
Because damn you've been working so hard.
But you're walking such a rough path
that you've seem to have chosen for yourself.

I think you've been running with the wrong crowd.
You never come back feeling any better
than you started off, worse even.

But I'll give them credit,
they validate your behavior
but not the sort that you
want to emulate,
only the worst.

I think you've been running with the wrong crowd
because damn you've been working so hard
but they don't see it like I do
and only want you to be on their plane.

I can see you're fighting their gravity
but it's pulling the worst part out from you.
Pulling the worst out of me.
I can't watch this any more

Pursuit

I chase my dreams
because my nightmares chase me.
I told you I loved you when
I was only twenty-eight.

And now I don't want this bottle to end
but in the end, I'll raise a glass for you.
And awakened I am,
maybe jaded, or maybe just numb.

I chase my by dreams
because my nightmares chase me
the past won't let me be
it's taken me out at the knees.

I told you I loved you when
I was only twenty-eight.
I hope I still can
but it might be too late.

Deep Fake

I didn't think this was possible
to date a deep fake
but here you are in front of me
proving my intuition
wrong.

I have to learn to
stand alone in
no man's land.

But instead living is
killing me.
And sometimes
I wish I would just let it
have the way it desires.

I fell in love
with a death machine
and it will never be enough
and I feel like it is heresy
just to be

Self Harm

My self-harm might be different than yours
but it's all the same
mine is just colorful
and passes as art
but it's all the same
only myself is to blame
for this pain
I inflict
on myself.

My self-harm might be different than yours
but covers the reality
all the same.
Such sweet entropy,
it's going to kill me.
And tonight
I'm losing control again
looking for another high
or is it a way out?
Would you turn
and let me go?
Or embrace me
and take it all away.
Just want another way to
fucking waste time

I'm just looking for a way out.

This should be fuckin' easy.

Care

It's always whatever
but I want you to care.
I want to pick up the mop
and clean up the past
but there isn't enough bleach
to make yours
not exist in the present.
Maybe I can lessen
it and take it out
of your fucked up mind.

It's always whatever
but I want you to care
and have some sort
of opinion
that isn't held in the back
of your muted mind.

I know that you're broken
a lot like me
so I thought we could fix each other
And I don't feel quite right
there must be something in the air tonight
Something is wrong
and you still don't care.

Someone Else

I always thought
it would be you leaving me
for someone else
but instead
here I am with my own plans.

Never did I think I would
be capable
of pulling a stunt like this
and it berates me
like a yellow jacket.

I don't think this will ever feel right
I told you I didn't want to hurt you
But I think I have to let you go
so you can be happy
with someone else.

I Don't Want to Have Any Regrets

I try and live with the mantra
there's no point in holding on to
regrets.
But here I am with so many.
I'm a hypocrite
asking you to forget your past
when the future scares
the shit out of me.

You look right through me
with those big brown eyes of yours
that I used to think held galaxies.

This is a mad world
I wish I could find it funny
the way you don't care at all

I don't want to have any regrets
and that's why I have to let you go
because I fear you'll never be happy
with me
as your own.

Disappointment

I know that if I do this,
I will disappoint myself
but if I don't
they will all be disappointed in me.

So I'll stay in the cyclical box
I've made for myself
and just be a sad sack of shit

What am I supposed to do?
Honestly?
No one can tell me the answer,
It's my life to live
and I can't decide.

I know that if I do this,
I will disappoint myself
but if I don't
they will all be disappointed in me.

There's so many of them,
is this what I want for myself?
They showed me what I expected
from a family
but is it enough
to accept this life?

If I bow out and run away
with my tail between my legs
like the coward you've made me
I'll become the disappointment
I feel inside.

Grace Period

There's a riot going in my head.
And they're all screaming for a decision.
But I can't make one,
so they just bellow louder.

There's a riot going in my head.
I just want it to end.
This cataclysm that's never coming
because I can't make up my mind.

There's a riot going in my head.
But I've made up my mind
and it grows no quieter
A small grace period I'll grant
just to see what you do
with it
with me.

Dear Diary

I wish I could ask you
to keep one.
Only just so I could peruse it
and figure you out.

You whom I thought
I wanted to spend my life with
has turned into a disguised siren
I can't even recognize.

If you found this you would cry
I think
but only in anger towards me
for not disclosing these thoughts
outloud.

So why can't I ask the same.
A simple composition,
a reading of you,
is all I want.

Voodoo Ranger

All I need is one
or seven
to forget this
misery
that paralyzes
the best in
me.

You tried to bend me until I break
but I'm the Voodoo Ranger
and I shattered instead.

Shambles on the floor
mixed with empty bottles
of pills and alcohol
all in attempts to find
normal.

All I need is one
or seven
to forget this
misery
that paralyzes
the best in
me.

I'm the Voodoo Ranger
charged with duty
to you
that I can't uphold.

My time is done.
I've hung my hat, all the while
wishing my own neck was there
instead.

When the Thoughts of You Pass

I realized something last night
at 0232.
I've lost all sight of my self.
The glasses are broken
and scratched,
from my own tantrums
in anger at my self.
A war I can't stop waging.

I realized something last night
at 0232.
I'm not who I was before.
My bones are broken, the muscles
frayed.
From your beatings,
only verbal
but thrice as hurtful.

I realized something last night
at 0232.
The thoughts of you passed
like a storm that raged
too long.
and I saw
with clarity
what I must do.

Splitting Hairs

Burn the pages
but you can't erase it
from my memory.
You can say
as many times as your please
you'll change
but I've given all I can
I am nothing left.

Tease

I've heard of your type
but never imagined it like this.

We started off one way
but then you flew your colors
and I saw what your bounty
really held.
It's time I hoist my own.

So here I am.
A tease all the same.
You're a monster
but so am I.

I'll confess my sins with a
sharp and pointed tongue.
So here I am,
the painter of your misery
all wrought by my mistakes.

Do I mend my mistakes?
And clean the canvas,
setting it all ablaze?

How do I apologize and
erase the tears from your eyes?
All I see are my failures.

You say good night
but I want to say goodbye.
And do you the service you deserve
But I can't
I can't
I can't

I'm a monster all the same.

A Subtle Green Tea

Here I lay
steeped in misery
nicotine
and alcohol.

Falling but still
following.
I can see the darkness
ever closer near.

Here I lay
steeped in misery
lithium
and hate.

Falling but still
crawling.
I could never taste your life
you were just a pawn
in my lost game.

Here I lay
steeped in misery
debt

and ink.

Falling but still
not yet dead.

Psychopathy

I feel nothing
I feel nothing
I feel nothing for you.

We sit and talk for hours
about our problems
and it's evident
that you won't change
so why should I?

Mis-communication
from someone that doesn't stop,
it all feels like a lie
and I feel nothing.

Off with my head you say,
off with my head
every time I don't say the right thing.
But how can I
when I feel nothing.

I didn't want this
but I thought you did
so now we're stuck

in a bind that
only ties us down,
and I feel nothing for you.

Wedding Bells

A sound I don't want to hear
but is coming anyway.
All I wanted was something simple
but we got carried away.

I wish I could take it back,
take away it all
but I can't
and we're a train hurtling towards bent rails.

You used to pull me out
of the endless night
I used to live in
but now you've placed me there
mercilessly.

Wedding bells,
a sound I don't want to hear
but here we are anyway
and I can't say no
because you said so.

Call It Off

That's it
I'm calling it off
we don't want this
and we shouldn't put ourselves in debt
for someone else.

Sure, I'll marry you
in a courthouse far from the family
that put us in this position
in the first place.

I'll take you to Vegas
and we can gamble the money
we would have spent
on a party for someone else.

I'll take you to the lake,
in the gown you bought for the ceremony
we don't believe in,
and marry you there.

I didn't want this
and neither did you
but here we are anyway

throwing a party for us
for someone else.

Sith

Do or do not
there is to try,
because I did.
I tried so hard
to make you happy.

But now I am dealing in absolutes;
hate
jealousy
and rage.

I can't stand without this spine.
You did this to me,
took my hand.
Nothing hurt more.

I wanted a life with you
but it felt forbidden
so I consumed myself
and wound up taking you
with me.

Now I'll done black
the only color that

doesn't lie.
Lashing out at the children
because I feel that will
be forced on me too.

Are you satisfied
with my death?

Ulysses

No one tied me to the mast
or stuffed wax about my ears
and now I've fallen.

You sang your song
and into the sea
I fell to chase after you.

They tried to tell me I was wrong
but not hard enough
and I wasn't listening
so I burned them all,
a viking funeral for my past,
all for you.

Around my finger
a knotted anchor
you wrought for me
and down I fell
once again into the sea.

Medusa

You are the pretty one
at least above the bone.
But I've seen what lies beneath,
under this disguise.

Turned to stone,
I can't move
away from you.

It's all pretty on the outside
but they don't see what happens
behind closed doors.

Tie me down
beat me bloody
it would be less agony
than what's coming.

06/02/2023

It is scheduled for September
but I just want this ember
to light this all ablaze.

I'll put it to you plain
I don't want this wedding.
Let me say this clearly
I think this is beyond mending.

We are trapped in a box.
Between your parents
and the banks.
They've closed both doors
and we can't break the locks.

We can't afford this
and never could.

We didn't want this
and never did.

We don't need this
and never will.

Yes it'd be nice
sure it'd be fun
but the sacrifice
made at the altar
is too grand.

Watching My World Burn

This isn't love
this is a sentence
and no one will post bail.

I have front row seats
to my own demise
handcuffed
and tied down.

I really want to change
but I can't learn from my mistakes
I really want to run
but I've shot out my own knees.

I'm circling the drain
just waiting to drop
so this can all be done.

You're fucking me up
and there's a part that's okay with that
but the rest bellows to end it all.

This isn't love,
this is a sentence.

Ease

I'm one with my mind
my mind is with me.
In one ear and out the other
this time I think I'll let this linger.

In the end I chose love
and that means you.
I can wake from this nightmare
I can escape this dark lair.

S.O.S.

I found me
when I found you.

Off with all my flares
you answered the call.

And now here we are
with futures in mind.

And I choose you today
I chose you yesterday
and I always will.
I can't throw this away.

I found me
when I found you.

And I can't wait
to see you dressed up in white
and finally call you mine.
I won't throw this away.

And I can't wait
to carry you across our threshold

into our future
together.

I imagined the thoughts of you
would pass.
But your siren song lingers on
and I pray it never ends.

Here's to you, my wife.
Awakened, I am.

Printed by BoD™in Norderstedt, Germany